X-TREME FACTS: CONTINENTS

OCEANIA

by Catherine C. Finan

BEARPORT
PUBLISHING

Minneapolis, Minnesota

Credits:

Title Page, 27 top, Martinmark/Dreamstime.com; 4–5, Simon_sees/Creative Commons; 4, Peter Hermes Furian | /Dreamstime.com; 5 top, Phillip Capper/Creative Commons; 5 middle, Klaus/Creative Commons; 5 bottom, Thurtell/iStock; 13 middle left, 13 bottom, 28 bottom left, ChameleonsEye/Shutterstock.com; 6, chujoslaw/Creative Commons; 6 top left, 10 top left, 12 top left, 13 bottom left, LightField Studios/Shutterstock; 6 top right, Prostock-studio/Shutterstock; 6 bottom, Petra/Creative Commons; 6 bottom middle, Anelo/Shutterstock; 6 bottom left, fizkes/Shutterstock; 7 top, Pi-Lens/Shutterstock; 7 top left, Brocreative/Shutterstock; 7 top middle, Olena Yakobchuk/Shutterstock; 7 middle left, gailhampshire/Creative Commons; 7 middle right, Christopher Michel/Creative Commons; 7 bottom, FiledIMAGE/Shutterstock; 7 bottom left, LittlePanda29/Shutterstock.com; 8–9,/LBM1948/Creative Commons; 8 middle, Thomas Gill/Shutterstock; 8 middle left, 8 middle right, 26 bottom, JJ Harrison/Creative Commons; 9 top, Joakant/Creative Commons; 9 top right, Sirrob01/Creative Commons; 9 middle, Krikkiat/Shutterstock; 9 bottom, chonlasub woravichan/Shutterstock; 9 bottom left, Luis Cristofori/Shutterstock; 9 bottom right, Denis Moskvinov/Shutterstock; 10 top, Corey Leopold/Creative Commons; 10 bottom, Schomynv/Public Domain; 11 top, Teckez/Creative Commons; 11 top left, Elena Nichizhenova/Shutterstock; 11 top middle, mahc/Shutterstock; 11 top right, rheins/Creative Commons; 11 middle left, Mark Marathon/Creative Commons; 11 middle right, Rhefford/Creative Commons; 11 bottom, Lucy Sgro/Creative Commons; 11 bottom left, gianni31 joker/Shutterstock; 11 bottom middle, Naveen Macro/Shutterstock.com; 12 top, Annette Teng/Creative Commons; 12 top middle, Vladislav T. Jirousek/Shutterstock.com; 12 right, Eric Isselee/Shutterstock; 13 top, ChameleonsEye/Shutterstock; 13 middle right, Krofoto/Shutterstock; 14 top, Fotos593/Shutterstock.com; 14 bottom, Joanne/Creative Commons; 14 bottom left, 22 top right, Roman Samborskyi/Shutterstock; 14 bottom middle, scott1346/Creative Commons; 15 top, Tony Hisgett/Creative Commons; 15 top right, Text and Tulip/Shutterstock.com; 15 middle left, Sarah Stewart/Creative Commons; 15 middle right, John Megahan/Creative Commons; 15 bottom, Phil Whitehouse/Creative Commons;/16 top, mimisim/Shutterstock; 16 top right, Bjørn Christian Tørrissen/Creative Commons; 16 bottom, Sid Mosdell/Creative Commons; 17 top, Hideaki Edo Photography/Shutterstock; 17 middle left, gérard/Creative Commons; 17 middle right, CraigL/Creative Commons; 17 bottom, Dean Weybury/Creative Commons; 17 bottom left, Joanna Nelson-Hauer/Shutterstock; 17 bottom right, franco schettini/Shutterstock; 18 top, SHIN-db/Shutterstock; 18 top left, Pics516/Dreamstime.com; 18 bottom, Ken Griffiths/Shutterstock; 19 upper top, Rosie Steinberg/Creative Commons; 19 top, Krzysztof Golik/Creative Commons; 19 top left, Michal Sloviak/Shutterstock; 19 top middle, Jukka Jantunen/Shutterstock; 19 top right, Dragon Images/Shutterstock; 19 middle right, Guido Gautsch/Creative Commons; 19 middle right, (c) 2005 Richard Ling/Creative Commons; 19 bottom, Tomas Kotouc/Shutterstock.com;/20 top, Francis Wheatley/Public Domain; 20, Algernon Talmage/Mitchell Library, State Library of New South Wales/Public Domain; 20 bottom left, Antonio Gravante/Shutterstock; 20 bottom right, Jim.henderson/Creative Commons; 21 top, ENRIQUE ALAEZ PEREZ/Shutterstock; 21 top right, Regine Poirier/Shutterstock; 21 middle left, Maksym Kozlenko/Creative Commons; 21 middle right, Sgt. William Holdaway/United States Marine Corps/Public Domain; 21 bottom, Radoslav Cajkovic/iStock; 22 top, Kgbo/Creative Commons; 22 top left, Jeka/Shutterstock; 22 bottom, DXR/Creative Commons; 23 top, Anton Leddin/Creative Commons;/23 top left, Fab_1/Shutterstock; 23 top right, GOLFX/Shutterstock; 23 middle left, T aro Taylor/Creative Commons; 23 middle right, Jérémie Silvestro/Wikimedia Commons/CC BY-SA 4.0 23 bottom, Kerry Raymond/Creative Commons; 23 bottom left, Twinsterphoto/Shutterstock; 23 bottom right, maroke/Shutterstock; 24 top, Johncarnemolla/Dreamstime.com; 24 top left, Dominic Jeanmaire/Shutterstock; 24 bottom, Georgy Dzyura/Dreamstime.com; 25 top, markaharper1/Creative Commons; 25 top left, Daniel Levitis/Creative Commons; 25 middle, Robert Whyte/Creative Commons; 25 bottom, Bernard Spragg/Creative Commons; 26 top, Squashem/Creative Commons;/27 top, Martinmark/Dreamstime.com; 27 top left, Juice Flair/Shutterstock; 27 middle, Tony Cannan/Creative Commons; 27 bottom, Coekon/Creative Commons; 27 bottom left, De Visu/Shutterstock; 28 top left, Frank Vincentz/Creative Commons; 28 top right, Kozak Sergii/Shutterstock; 28 middle right, Rob Hyrons/Shutterstock; 28 bottom right, Nai_Pisage/Shutterstock; 29, Austen Photography

Bearport Publishing Company Product Development Team

President: Jen Jenson; Director of Product Development: Spencer Brinker; Managing Editor: Allison Juda; Associate Editor: Naomi Reich; Associate Editor: Tiana Tran; Senior Designer: Colin O'Dea; Designer: Elena Klinkner; Designer: Kayla Eggert; Product Development Assistant: Owen Hamlin

Produced for Bearport Publishing by BlueAppleWorks Inc.

Managing Editor for BlueAppleWorks: Melissa McClellan; Art Director: T.J. Choleva; Photo Research: Jane Reid

STATEMENT ON USAGE OF GENERATIVE ARTIFICIAL INTELLIGENCE

Bearport Publishing remains committed to publishing high-quality nonfiction books. Therefore, we restrict the use of generative AI to ensure accuracy of all text and visual components pertaining to a book's subject. See BearportPublishing.com for details.

Library of Congress Cataloging-in-Publication Data

Names: Finan, Catherine C., 1972- author.
Title: Oceania / by Catherine C. Finan.
Description: Minneapolis, Minnesota : Bearport Publishing, [2024] | Series: X-treme facts : continents | Includes bibliographical references and index.
Identifiers: LCCN 2023031463 (print) | LCCN 2023031464 (ebook) | ISBN 9798889164340 (hardcover) | ISBN 9798889164425 (paperback) | ISBN 9798889164494 (ebook)
Subjects: LCSH: Oceania--Juvenile literature.
Classification: LCC DU17 .F56 2024 (print) | LCC DU17 (ebook) | DDC 995--dc23/eng/20230721
LC record available at https://lccn.loc.gov/2023031463
LC ebook record available at https://lccn.loc.gov/2023031464

Copyright © 2024 Bearport Publishing Company. All rights reserved. No part of this publication may be reproduced in whole or in part, stored in any retrieval system, or transmitted in any form or by any means, electronic, mechanical, photocopying, recording, or otherwise, without written permission from the publisher.

For more information, write to Bearport Publishing, 5357 Penn Avenue South, Minneapolis, MN 55419.

Contents

Destination: Oceania 4
Astonishing Landscapes 6
The (Very!) Great Barrier Reef 8
Uluru 10
The World's Oldest Living Culture 12
The Magnificent Māori 14
You're So Unique! 16
Oh-So-Deadly Animals 18
An Interesting Past 20
Spectacular Cities, Sensational Spots 22
Kooky Stuff in the Land Down Under 24
Your Own Oceania Adventure 26

Build a Boomerang 28
Glossary 30
Read More 31
Learn More Online 31
Index 32
About the Author 32

Destination: Oceania

Imagine a **continent** that's surrounded by ocean yet is best known for scorching deserts and towering volcanoes. Here, you'll find animals that don't exist anywhere else in the world. There's also a **coral reef** so huge it's visible from space. You're imagining Oceania! This continent is made up of Australia, New Zealand, New Guinea, and thousands of smaller islands throughout the Pacific Ocean. There's so much to explore!

There are more than 25,000 islands in the Pacific Ocean. Many of them are part of Oceania.

Oceania is broken into 4 regions. They are called Australasia, Micronesia, Melanesia, and Polynesia.

Australia has three times as many sheep as people. But New Zealand beats that, with nearly five sheep to every person.

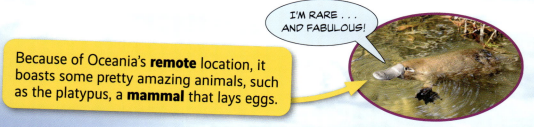

Because of Oceania's **remote** location, it boasts some pretty amazing animals, such as the platypus, a **mammal** that lays eggs.

Oceania is home to thousands of **Indigenous** groups. **The Aboriginal peoples of Australia are the largest Indigenous group on the continent.**

Astonishing Landscapes

If you travel across Oceania, you might be surprised at just how many different landscapes there are to see. The continent features everything from sunny coastal beaches and tropical rain forests to barren deserts and snow-capped mountains. Be sure to pack your suitcase wisely. A tour of Oceania requires clothes that can keep up with the changing conditions!

The middle part of Australia **is covered in an open area of land called the Outback.**

OUT BACK OF WHERE?

THIS SAYS WE'RE IN THE OUTBACK.

C'MON, LET'S GO VISIT ANOTHER BEACH.

DO WE HAVE TO? AFTER 25 YEARS THEY ALL START TO LOOK THE SAME!

Australia has about 10,000 different beaches along its coasts. You could visit a new beach every day for more than 27 years.

Long ago, volcanoes created New Zealand's two main islands. Some of these volcanoes are still active today.

I TOLD YOU THAT VOLCANO IS ACTIVE!

GET READY FOR *NEW* NEW ZEALAND!

New Guinea has Earth's third-largest rain forest. It contains about 5 percent of Earth's plant and animal **species**.

The Marshall Islands were formed by underwater volcanoes rising above the ocean's surface.

OCEANIA HAS IT ALL!

The Australian Alps get more snow than Europe's more famous Swiss Alps.

7

The (Very!) Great Barrier Reef

Want to visit something big in Oceania? Try the Great Barrier Reef. This natural wonder off the coast of Australia is the largest living structure on Earth! It is made up of many smaller reefs that are formed from tiny sea animals called coral polyps. Over time, polyps use material from seawater to make hard outer skeletons that protect their soft bodies. Let's dive down to learn more!

The Great Barrier Reef is a system of 3,000 separate reefs.

I'M TIRED. LET'S LAND SOMEWHERE TO REST A WHILE.

TAKE YOUR PICK OF REEFS!

The Great Barrier Reef stretches for 1,400 miles (2,300 km). That's longer than the country of Italy.

Uluru

Uluru is another one of Oceania's famous sites. This huge rock in central Australia towers above the flat desert surrounding it. It's impressive at any time of day, but the formation takes on a fiery glow at sunset. The history inside is just as exciting. Caves at Uluru's base are **sacred** to Aboriginal peoples who have been in the area for more than 30,000 years. Paintings and carvings inside the caves tell their story of creation.

Uluru rises 1,100 feet (300 m) **above** the desert around it.

IT'S SO BIG!

WHAT YOU SEE IS ONLY THE TIP OF THE ICEBERG . . . I MEAN ROCK!

Uluru's rocky base reaches 1.5 miles (2.5 km) underground.

The creation story of Aboriginal peoples in this area is called the Dreaming. In it, Aboriginal **ancestors** came to Earth **and created everything.**

Uluru gets its color from iron rusting within the rock's sandstone.

THAT COLOR LOOKS GREAT ON YOU!

THANKS. I MAKE IT MYSELF!

After rainstorms, gushing waterfalls sometimes crash over the massive rock's cliffs.

Tiny **crustaceans** called shield shrimp hatch in pools that form on Uluru after heavy rains.

In summer, temperatures at Uluru can reach a sizzling 116 degrees Fahrenheit (47 degrees Celsius).

LET'S TAKE A WALK AROUND THIS ROCK.

IN THIS HEAT? LET'S GO INTO A CAVE INSTEAD.

The path around the rock is almost 6 miles (10 km) long.

11

The World's Oldest Living Culture

Aboriginal peoples have lived on Australia for nearly 65,000 years. This makes them Earth's oldest living culture. And they aren't Oceania's only group of Indigenous peoples. Torres Strait Islanders have lived on islands off the northern coast for thousands of years. While they have their own unique cultures, both groups value the land, living things, and water in their homelands.

There were once more than 250 different Aboriginal languages. About 150 of them are still spoken.

More than 400 words in the English language—including *koala*, *kangaroo*, and *boomerang*—come from Aboriginal languages.

Torres Strait Islanders believe an ancient fisherman called Tagai created the world. Many of their ways of life are based on stories of him.

The didgeridoo is one of Earth's oldest instruments! Aboriginal peoples create it from hollowed-out tree limbs.

Thousands of years ago, Aboriginal peoples invented the boomerang to hunt animals.

Aboriginal peoples use a style of dot painting to keep sacred **symbols** hidden from outsiders. The dots cover symbols beneath.

WOW! COOL MASKS!

OUR WHOLE CULTURE IS COOL, KID!

Today, some Aboriginal and Torres Strait Islanders practice the same **rituals** and ceremonies that their ancestors did thousands of years ago.

13

The Magnificent Māori

The first people to live on New Zealand were the Māori. According to their history, the Māori arrived at the islands in a large fleet of canoes about 700 years ago. The word *Māori* may mean ordinary people, but Māori culture is extraordinary! These people keep their rich history alive through storytelling, dancing, and carving artwork, among other things.

One way Māori people may greet each other is by pressing their foreheads and noses together.

Haka are a variety of famous Māori dances that include stomping, shouting, and making fierce faces. Groups perform them during special occasions.

The Māori are known for their terrific tattoos. Each one is unique and tells a person's family history.

Hundreds of years ago, the Māori used sharpened animal bones to put tattoo ink under the skin. This is sometimes still done today.

A traditional Māori food called Hāngī' is cooked in an underground pit using heated rocks.

The earliest Māori were called the Moa Hunters after the moa bird they hunted.

Whakairo is the Māori art of carving wood, stone, and bone. The carved symbols show parts of Māori history.

You're So Unique!

Oceania has some of the most unique animals on Earth. Why is that? The large landmasses and smaller islands that make up the continent broke away from the rest of Earth's land millions of years ago. Separated from the rest of the world by vast waters, animals in Oceania adapted differently.

Wombats mark their territory with cube-shaped poop! Scientists think this special shape keeps the poop in place so other wombats steer clear.

The tuatara is a lizardlike reptile found only in New Zealand. The reptiles that were most closely related to it went **extinct** 60 million years ago.

Oh-So-Deadly Animals

With so many unique animals, it's no surprise that the continent is also home to some of the deadliest creatures in the world. Poisonous fish, **venomous** jellyfish, and fierce sharks swim in the open ocean. On land, look out for dangerous spiders and snakes. It's time to meet some of Oceania's deadliest creatures . . . if you dare!

Although the blue-ringed octopus is only the size of a golf ball, its venom is extremely deadly.

Australia's inland taipan is the world's most venomous snake. The venom in one bite could kill 100 people.

The cassowary is considered Earth's most dangerous bird. The creatures use their 4-inch (10-cm) **talons** on anything that comes too close.

Great white sharks are the largest hunting fish in the ocean.

An Interesting Past

The first Europeans to set up a **colony** on Australia weren't the best of the bunch. In 1788, a British ship full of prisoners arrived. Having already filled up its own prisons, the Brits sent their extra criminals to Australia. Soon, more prisoners and free settlers arrived, and the colony grew. Britain claimed Australia, New Zealand, and other Pacific islands as their own, even though Indigenous peoples already lived there. Oceania's population grew with colonists, crooks, and criminals.

British officer Arthur Phillip commanded the original 11 prison ships from Britain to Australia. He became the colony's first governor.

I BROUGHT THE FIRST FLEET IN!

Prisoners were forced to clear the land for farming. Many struggled to survive in the harsh climate.

LET'S CELEBRATE THE BRITISH BEING IN AUSTRALIA!

YOU PRISONERS ARE HERE TO WORK, NOT TO CELEBRATE!

BUT WE BUILT THE PLACE!

Today, there are 14 independent countries and 11 territories in Oceania.

The Dutch reached New Guinea in 1828, claiming the western part of the island. The British took control of the southeastern part in 1884.

Fiji, a country in the South Pacific that is made up of 300 islands, was also once a British colony. It became an independent country in 1970.

Samoa is one of the smallest countries in the world. It was once a territory of New Zealand but gained independence in 1962.

Spectacular Cities, Sensational Spots

Today, Oceania is a vast region in the Pacific with a mix of different people, cultures, and lifestyles. The continent's biggest cities are found in Australia and New Zealand. But the smaller villages and towns dotting the beautiful tropical islands of Micronesia, Melanesia, and Polynesia are just as sensational. There's so much to experience on an epic journey through Oceania.

Oceania's five most populated cities are all in Australia.

Nearly 90 percent of Australians live in cities.

Auckland is New Zealand's largest city. It's also home to more than 50 volcanoes.

People in the village of Navala, Fiji, live in traditional homes called bures. These are built with natural materials, such as wood and straw.

The small city of Papeete is found on the island of Tahiti. It's the capital of French Polynesia.

From the town of Rabaul in Papua New Guinea, you can watch active volcanoes at Rabaul Volcano Observatory.

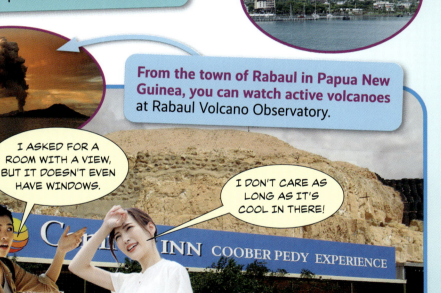

The town of Coober Pedy is in Australia's blazing-hot outback. More than half its residents escape the heat by living underground in abandoned **opal** mines.

23

Kooky Stuff in the Land Down Under

Oceania is full of wild facts too extreme to forget! Did you know giant birds called thunderbirds roamed Australia about 40,000 years ago? They were 10 ft (3 m) tall and weighed 1,100 pounds (500 kg). And New Zealand is home to a hill with a Māori name that's 85 letters long. In Tahiti, what look like mailboxes outside people's homes are actually for bread deliveries. What a wild and wonderful place!

I JUST WANT DINNER. CAN'T YOU CUT A DOG A BREAK?

Australia's Dingo Fence is the world's longest fence. It was built to keep Australia's native dogs away from sheep.

When a U.S. space station crashed in Western Australia, a nearby town fined NASA $400 for littering. NASA never paid!

The world championship for cockroach-racing is held every year in Brisbane, Australia.

I WAS LAST YEAR'S CHAMPION!

24

Ever heard of a poisonous bird? **Papua New Guinea's hooded pitohui has poisonous skin and feathers.**

The community of Kiwirrkurra in western Australia is closer to space than it is to the next nearest town.

The Great Barrier Reef has its own mailbox! It's on a reef 45 miles (70 km) off the coast of Port Douglas, Australia.

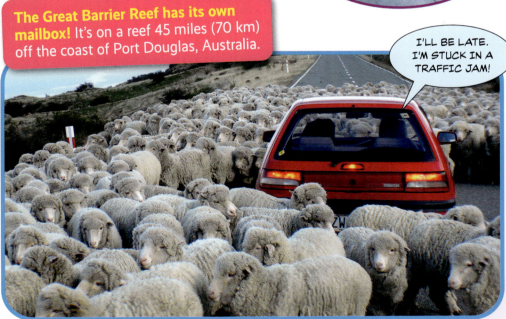

New Zealand is home to more than 25 million sheep.

Your Own Oceania Adventure

Oceania is made up of thousands of islands with beautiful features, unique wildlife, and amazing cultures. You would have to cover nearly 38 million square miles (100 million square km) to visit every corner of this remote place. Whether you are in a bustling city, on a sandy beach, or in the scorching desert, there is so much left to explore! What incredible sights will you see on this extreme continent?

New Zealand's Blue Lake has crystal clear water unlike any other lake on Earth.

I HAVE THE CLEAREST WATER!

WHAT A BREATH OF FRESH AIR!

Australia's island of Tasmania lies off the country's southeast coast. **It has some of the cleanest air in the world!**

26

Motu Tapu is a small island near the island of Bora Bora. It's thought to be the most photographed place in the South Pacific.

You might see the aurora australis, or southern lights, in the night sky. These colorful light shows happen when energy particles from the sun hit Earth's **atmosphere**.

The Sydney Opera House in Australia has a roof shaped like boat sails. It was inspired by the many sailboats in Sydney Harbor.

Build a Boomerang
Craft Project

The boomerang is very important to Australia's Aboriginal peoples. It is not only a hunting tool, but also a part of their creation story. Aboriginal Australians believe their ancestors threw boomerangs into the earth, creating mountains, rocks, and rivers. You can craft your own boomerang by following these easy steps.

The oldest Aboriginal boomerangs ever found are 10,000 years old.

What You Will Need
- Cardstock
- A pencil
- Scissors
- An eraser
- A black marker
- Crayons

Boomerangs can also be used as instruments. They're sometimes rattled together to make music during ceremonial dances.

Step One

Draw the shape of a boomerang on the cardstock.

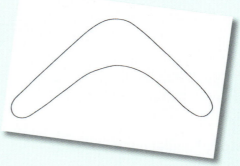

Step Two

Using scissors, carefully cut out the boomerang shape. Erase any pencil marks that are still showing.

Step Three

With a black marker, draw large shapes on the boomerang. These can be circles, wavy lines, dots, or anything else you might like.

Step Four

Use crayons to decorate the boomerang. Color between and around all the marker shapes.

Glossary

algae tiny plantlike living things that grow in ponds, lakes, rivers, and oceans

ancestors family members who lived long ago

atmosphere the layer of gases surrounding Earth

climate change changes in the usual weather patterns around Earth, including the warming of the air and oceans

colony an area that has been settled by people from another country and is ruled by that country

continent one of Earth's seven large landmasses

coral reef a group of structures formed from the skeletons of sea animals called coral polyps

crustaceans animals with hard shells and no backbone, such as crabs, lobsters, and shrimp

extinct when a kind of plant or animal dies out completely

Indigenous originally from a place, including the peoples in an area

mammal an animal that usually has hair or fur, gives birth to live young, and drinks milk from its mother as a baby

marsupials groups of animals in which mothers have pouches on their bodies to carry their young

opal a kind of mineral that is often used as a gem

remote far away or difficult to reach

rituals special ceremonies for religious or other purposes

sacred very important or holy

species groups that animals are divided into, according to similar characteristics

symbols objects or pictures that stand for something else

talons sharp, curved claws on the feet of some kinds of birds

venomous full of poison that can be delivered by a bite or sting

Read More

Doeden, Matt. *Travel to Australia (World Traveler).* Minneapolis: Lerner Publications, 2022.

Harts, Shannon H. *The Geography of Australia and the Pacific Realm (Explore the World).* New York: The Rosen Publishing Group, Inc., 2021.

Prior, Jennifer. *Oceania.* Huntington Beach, CA: Teacher Created Materials Inc., 2023.

Learn More Online

1. Go to **www.factsurfer.com** or scan the QR code below.

2. Enter **"X-treme Oceania"** into the search box.

3. Click on the cover of this book to see a list of websites.

Index

Aboriginal peoples 5, 10, 12–13, 28
ancestors 10, 13, 28
boomerang 12–13, 28–29
coral 4, 8–9
Dreaming 10
Fiji 21, 23
Great Barrier Reef 8–9, 25
mammals 5, 17
Māori people 14–15, 24
marsupials 17
Melanesia 22
Micronesia 22
New Guinea 7, 21
New Zealand 4–5, 7, 14, 16, 20, 22, 24–26
outback 6, 23
Papua New Guinea 23, 25
Polynesia 4, 22–23, 27
prison colony 20
Tahiti 23–24
Torres Strait Islander peoples 12–13
Uluru 10–12
volcanoes 4, 7, 22–23

About the Author

Catherine C. Finan is a writer living in northeastern Pennsylvania. Her dream vacation is a trip to Bora Bora. Maybe someday!